Sing a Song of
MOTHER
GOOSE

BARBARA REID

North Winds Press

An Imprint of Scholastic Canada Ltd.

The illustrations in this book were made with Plasticine
that is shaped and pressed onto illustration board.

The text type was set in 24 point Esprit Book.

Photography by Ian Crysler.

Library and Archives Canada Cataloguing in Publication

Sing a song of Mother Goose / illustrated by Barbara Reid.

ISBN 978-0-545-99028-8

1. Nursery rhymes. I. Reid, Barbara, 1957-
PZ8.3.M85Si 2008   j398.8   C2008-900896-0

ISBN-10 0-545-99028-9

6 5 4 3 2 1   Printed in Singapore   08 09 10 11 12 13

To W. H. for all the fun!
— B.R.

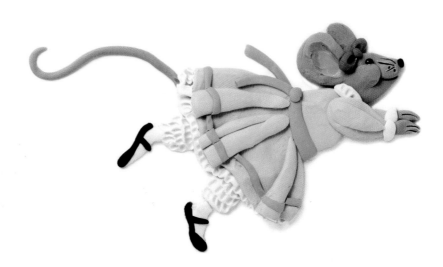

Sing a Song

Sing a song of sixpence,
A pocket full of rye;
Four and twenty blackbirds
Baked in a pie!

When the pie was opened
The birds began to sing;
Wasn't that a dainty dish
To set before the king?

Jack and Jill

Jack and Jill
Went up the hill,
To fetch a pail of water;
Jack fell down
And broke his crown,
And Jill came tumbling after.

Hey Diddle, Diddle

Hey diddle diddle,
The cat and the fiddle,
The cow jumped over the moon;
The little dog laughed
To see such sport,
And the dish ran away
with the spoon.

Ladybug

Ladybug, ladybug,
  fly away home!
Your house is on fire,
  your children all gone;
All but one,
  and her name is Ann,
And she crept under
  the pudding pan.

Mary Had a Little Lamb

Mary had a little lamb,
Its fleece was white as snow;
And everywhere that Mary went
The lamb was sure to go.

It followed her to school one day,
Which was against the rules;
It made the children laugh and play
To see a lamb at school.

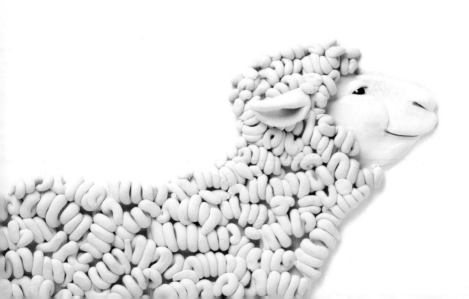

Humpty Dumpty

Humpty Dumpty
    sat on a wall,
Humpty Dumpty
    had a great fall;
All the King's horses
    and all the King's men
Couldn't put Humpty
    together again.

Baa, Baa, Black Sheep

Baa, baa, black sheep,
Have you any wool?
Yes, sir, yes, sir,
Three bags full;
One for the master,
One for the dame,
And one for the little boy
Who lives down the lane.

Pat-a-Cake

Pat-a-cake, pat-a-cake,
Baker's man!
Bake me a cake
As fast as you can.
Pat it, and prick it,
And mark it with B,
Put it in the oven
For baby and me.

Pussy Cat, Pussy Cat

Pussy cat, pussy cat,
Where have you been?
I've been to London
To visit the queen.
Pussy cat, pussy cat,
What did you there?
I frightened a little mouse
Under her chair.

Rock-a-bye Baby

Rock-a-bye baby,
On the tree top,
When the wind blows
The cradle will rock;
When the bough breaks
The cradle will fall,
And down will come baby,
Cradle, and all.

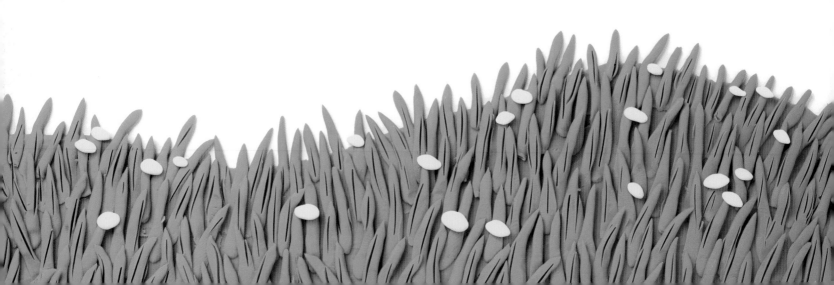

Rain

Rain, rain, go away,
Come again another day;
Little Johnny wants to play.

Little Miss Muffet

Little Miss Muffet
Sat on a tuffet,
Eating her curds and whey;
There came a big spider,
Who sat down beside her
And frightened Miss Muffet away.

Hickory, Dickory, Dock

Hickory, dickory, dock,
The mouse ran up the clock.
The clock struck one,
The mouse ran down,
Hickory, dickory, dock.

Twinkle, Twinkle, Little Star

Twinkle, twinkle, little star,
How I wonder what you are!
Up above the world so high,
Like a diamond in the sky.

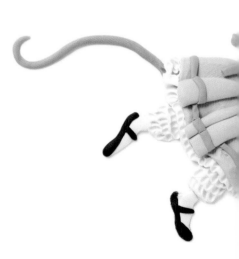